D1201395

DC SUPER HEROES
SCHOOL JOKES

BY MICHAEL DAHL
& DONALD LEMKE

STONE ARCH BOOKS
a capstone imprint

Published by Capstone Young Readers in 2018
A Capstone Imprint
1710 Roe Crest Drive
North Mankato, Minnesota 56003
www.capstonepub.com

STAR39966

Cataloging-in-Publication Data is available on the
Library of Congress website.

ISBN: 978-1-4965-5761-2 (library hardcover)
ISBN: 978-1-4965-5765-0 (eBook)

Summary: Why did Wonder Woman study in her Invisible Jet?
She wanted a higher education! This official DC Comics joke book
features laugh-out-loud jokes about SCHOOL.

Designer: Brann Garvey

Printed in the United States
214

HA!
HA!
HA!

HA!
HA!
HA!

HA!
HA!
HA!

HA!
HA!
HA!

Why did Superman go to
the school baseball game?
**He'd heard someone
had stolen a base.**

What did Cyborg tell the math student?
"You can count on me!"

Why did Metallo go to
the school nurse?
**He wasn't getting
enough iron.**

Why did Aquaman get an
A in music class?
**He was great at
conducting orca-stras.**

Why did Superman sit on
the school's roof?

He wanted to be
in high school!

Why did Krypto sleep
under the bus at night?
**He wanted to
wake up oily
for school!**

How do you stop
Super-Dog from barking in
the back of the bus?
**Put him in the
front of the bus.**

What did Superman say when he couldn't
pass his algebra test?
"Clark can't!"

Why was Superman so good at subtraction?

He knows how to carry all those numerals!

Why was Lois Lane so good at organizing her homework?
Because she'd daily plan it!

What vegetable did Supergirl eat in the library?
Quiet peas!

Why did Supergirl wear lipstick to history class?
They were having a make-up exam!

Why did Cyborg spend all his time
in the cafeteria?

**He wanted
more bytes!**

Why did Cyborg pack fish for lunch?

**Because it goes good
with micro-chips!**

Why did Black Manta throw all the
library books into the ocean?

**He wanted to make
a title wave.**

Why did Wonder Woman study
in her Invisible Jet?

**She wanted a
higher education!**

Why did the teacher send Wonder Woman
home as soon as she arrived at school?
**Because she still had
her paj-Amazon!**

Where does Superman travel
through time?

**The cafeteria —
because he always
goes back for seconds.**

Where does Doomsday sit
in math class?

**Anywhere he
wants to!**

Why did the Penguin get a penalty
during basketball practice?

For fowl play.

Why did the teacher make
Robin sit in the corner?

He said a bat word!

Why did Robin ask Batman
to join the school choir?

To perform a
Dynamic Duet!

What do you get when you cross a
calculator with the Dark Knight?
A cal-crusader.

What is the Dark Knight's favorite
thing he learned in school?
The alpha-bat!

What do you get when
you cross the Dark Knight
with a math teacher?
A bat-matician!

Why did young billionaire Bruce Wayne never get in trouble at school?

He always had the most cents.

Why did Robin bring a cake to school?
It was his bird-day!

What did Robin make in art class?
A bat-mobile.

What did the Joker
shout when he
jumped out of the
janitor's closet?
"Supplies!"

Why was the Joker kicked off the baseball team?
He kept stealing second base.

What bird does the Penguin always
bring to the cafeteria?
A swallow.

What happened
when Harley Quinn
joined theater
class?

**She stole
the show!**

What school subject does Poison Ivy like the best?
Geome-tree!

What is Poison Ivy's favorite
grade level?
Kinder-garden.

Why is math Poison Ivy's
least favorite subject?
**Because she
hates square
roots.**

Was Poison Ivy able to climb
the rope in gym class?
**Yes, she climbed
up itch by itch!**

Why won't Catwoman
use a computer?
**She's afraid
she'll eat the
mouse!**

What is Catwoman's favorite
school subject?
Mew-sic.

How is music class like Killer Croc?
They both have scales.

Why is Two-Face good at gymnastics?
He has a splits personality!

Why was the Penguin sent to the principal's office?
He was using fowl language!

What does
Mr. Freeze like best
about school?

**Snow
and tell!**

Why is Hawkman so good
in debate class?

**Because he has such
strong pinions about
everything.**

Why did Wonder Woman fly
her jet to music class?

**So she could reach
the high notes.**

What language class does
The Flash take?

Rushin'!

What is Elastic Lad's
after-school activity?

**He practices with
the rubber band!**

Did Bouncing Boy have a
good year at school?

It was up and down.

Why did Plastic Man wear
sunglasses to school?

**Because he was
so bright!**

How does Bumblebee get to school?
By school buzz!

Why did the Atom need a ladder
for school choir?
**To reach the
high notes!**

What happened when the Invisible Kid
lied about his report card?
**His parents could see
right through him.**

Why did Starro join the
debate team?
**He was good at
making points.**

How could you tell Martian Manhunter
didn't like the food in the cafeteria?
His face was green!

Why was Martian Manhunter
so good in Kinder-garden?
**He had a
green thumb!**

What school sport is Green Lantern
the best at?

Boxing – all his power
is in the ring!

What should you do if Green Lantern
forgets to set his alarm for school?
Give him a ring!

What is Hal Jordan's favorite schoolyard game?

Rings Around the Rosie.

What is Zatanna's favorite school subject? **Spell-ing.**

What did the art teacher get when she crossed Green Lantern with Aquaman? **Teal!**

Can Superman jump higher than a school building? **Of course he can, buildings can't jump!**

What do you get when you cross
Cyborg with a gym teacher?
A Cy-Ed Instructor!

Why does Beast Boy turn
into a dog at lunch?
It's chow time!

How does the teacher feel whenever
Superboy leaves the classroom?
She sees red.

Why did the math teacher sit in
Wonder Woman's Invisible Jet?
**She wanted her
lesson to be clear!**

What does Hawkman do when he forgets to study for a test?

He wings it!

Why did Bumblebee get sent to the principal's office?

For chewing bumble-gum.

Why did the teacher give Hawkman an F on the test?

He was caught cheeping!

Why was Hawkwoman excited to go back to school?

She heard they built a new wing!

WHY DID THE FLASH SPEND SO MUCH TIME IN THE LIBRARY?

Because he was, well, red!

Why is Aquaman so smart?
Because fish spend a lot of time in schools.

How does Aqualad help
the music teacher?
He knows how to
tuna piano!

What do you call Jumpa's
school uniform?
A jump-suit.

Why did Starro quit teaching?
He only had
one pupil!

Why was it so hard for Aqualad
to get an A on the test?

**His grades were
always below C-level!**

What was the Penguin's
favorite meal in school?

Ice-burgers.

What did Aquaman use to build a
school building under the ocean?

SEA-ment.

What did the nurse give
Swamp Thing when he felt sick?

Plenty of room!

WHY DOESN'T THE FLASH EAT IN THE SCHOOL CAFETERIA?

He prefers fast food!

What's Titano's favorite
school sport?
Squash!

What do you get when you cross
a teacher with Gorilla Grodd?
**I don't know, but
you better behave
in its class!**

Why did Glomulus eat the exam paper?
The teacher told him it would be a piece of cake.

What was Glomulus' favorite number?
Ate!

What do you call a Bizarro backpack?
A frontpack.

What do you get when you cross
Bizarro with a teacher?
A teach-him!

Why did Bizarro bury
his math book?
**He wanted to grow
smarter!**

What did Cheetah say after lunch?
**"That sure hit
the spots!"**

When is Darkseid like a school supply?
When he's a ruler.

What kind of dog does Lex Luthor
take to science class?
A lab!

During which school period does Lex
Luthor put his robots together?
Assembly!

I DON'T FEEL WELL.

WHO WENT TO THE
SCHOOL NURSE'S OFFICE?

CLARK KENT – HE WASN'T FEELING SUPER!

CATWOMAN – SHE WAS FELINE BAD!

THE JOKER – HE FELT FUNNY ALL OVER!

BRUCE WAYNE – HE HAD A BAT COLD!

THE FLASH
- HE WAS
RUNNING A
FEVER!

HAWKMAN - HE HAD THE FLEW!

MARTIAN MANHUNTER - HE WAS LOOKING GREEN!

AQUAMAN – HE HAD A SPLITTING HADDOCK!

THE ATOM – BUT HE ONLY HAD A LITTLE PAIN!

What after-school activity is
The Flash the best at?

Darts.

What happened when the Joker
stole a calendar off the
teacher's desk?

**He got
twelve months.**

Why did The Flash take a human
anatomy class?

**Because he's a
zoomin', of course!**

What does Krypto eat at snack time?

Pup-corn!

HOW DID THE FLASH FINISH HIS READING ASSIGNMENT SO QUICKLY?

He raced through all the chapters and dashed off a report!

Why did The Flash wear a helmet
in the school lunchroom?

He was on a
crash diet!

Why did The Flash go to the
school nurse's office?

He was feeling
run down!

Why did The Flash's classmates in school like him so much?

He was good at making fast friends.

HOW TO TELL JOKES!

1. KNOW the joke.
Make sure you remember the whole joke before you tell it. This sounds like a no-brainer, but most of us have known someone who says, "Oh, this is so funny . . ." Then, when they tell the joke, they can't remember the end. And that's the whole point of a joke – its punch line.

2. SPEAK CLEARLY.
Don't mumble; don't speak too fast or too slow. Just speak like you normally do. You don't have to use a different voice or accent or sound like someone else.

3. LOOK at your audience.
Good eye contact with your listeners will grab their attention.

4. DON'T WORRY about gestures or how to stand or sit when you tell your joke. Remember, telling a joke is basically talking.

5. DON'T LAUGH at your own joke.
Yeah, yeah, I know some comedians break up while they're acting in a sketch or telling a story, but the best rule to follow is not to laugh. If you start to laugh, you might lose the rhythm of your joke or keep yourself from telling the joke clearly. Let your audience laugh. That's their job. Your job is to be the funny one.

6. THE PUNCH LINE is the most important part of the joke.

It's the climax, the payoff, the main event. A good joke can sound even better if you pause for just a second or two before you deliver the punch line. That tiny pause will make your audience mentally sit up and hold their breath, eager to hear what's coming next.

7. The SETUP is the second most important part of a joke.

That's basically everything you say before you get to the punch line. And that's why you need to be as clear as you can (see 2) so that when you finally reach the punch line, it makes sense!

8. YOU CAN GET FUNNIER.

It's easy. Watch other comedians. Listen to other people tell a joke or story. Check out a good comedy show or film. You can pick up some skills simply by seeing how others get their comedy across. You will absorb it! And soon it will come naturally.

9. Last, but not least, telling a joke is all about TIMING.

That means not only getting the biggest impact for your joke, waiting for the right time, giving that extra pause before the punch line — but it also means knowing when NOT to tell a joke. When you're among friends, you can tell when they'd like to hear something funny. But in an unfamiliar setting, get a "sense of the room" first. Are people having a good time? Or is it a more serious event? A joke has the most funny power when it's told in the right setting.

MICHAEL DAHL

Michael Dahl is the prolific author of the bestselling *Goodnight, Baseball* picture book and more than 200 other books for children and young adults. He has won the AEP Distinguished Achievement Award three times for his nonfiction, a Teacher's Choice award from *Learning* magazine, and a Seal of Excellence from the Creative Child Awards. And he has won awards for his board books for the earliest learners, *Duck Goes Potty* and *Bear Says "Thank You!"* Dahl has written and edited numerous graphic novels for younger readers, authored the Library of Doom adventure series, the Dragonblood books, Trollhunters, and the Hocus Pocus Hotel mystery/comedy series. Dahl has spoken at schools, libraries, and conferences across the US and the UK, including ALA, AASL, IRA, and Renaissance Learning. He currently lives in Minneapolis, Minnesota, in a haunted house.

DONALD LEMKE

Donald Lemke works as a children's book editor. He has written dozens of all-age comics and children's books for Capstone, HarperCollins, Running Press, and more. Donald lives in St. Paul, Minnesota, with his brilliant wife, Amy, two toddling toddlers, and a not-so-golden retriever named Paulie.

JOKE DICTIONARY!

bit (BIT)—a section of a comedy routine

comedian (kuh-MEE-dee-uhn)—an entertainer who makes people laugh

headliner (HED-lye-ner)—the last comedian to perform in a show

improvisation (im-PRAH-vuh-ZAY-shuhn)—a performance that hasn't been planned; "improv" for short

lineup (LINE-uhp)—a list of people who are going to perform in a show

one-liner (WUHN-lye-ner)—a short joke or funny remark

open mike (OH-puhn MIKE)—an event at which anyone can use the microphone to perform for the audience

punch line (PUHNCH line)—the words at the end of a joke that make it funny or surprising

shtick (SHTIK)—a repetitive, comic performance or routine

segue (SEG-way)—a sentence or phrase that leads from one joke or routine to another

stand-up (STAND-uhp)—the type of comedy performed while standing alone on stage

timing (TIME-ing)—the use of rhythm and tempo to make a joke funnier

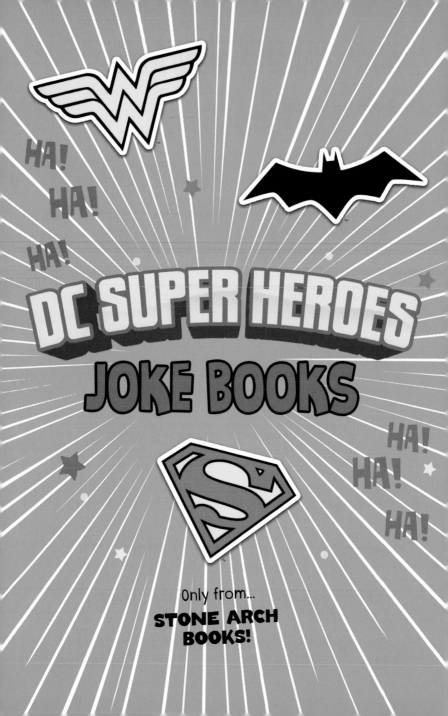